Editors Note

I'm bringing spooky back!

Well, that is what I have been telling people when they ask why I'm running Paracon Australia. Here we are year two and with many lessons learned ready to rock and paranormal roll. This time in one of my favourite places on earth, The Blue Mountains, in particular The Carrington Hotel. Bringing to life Paracon Australia is Frankenstein style effort and I am simply not capable of producing all this awesomeness by myself and it wouldn't have happen if I didn't have the blood, sweat and tears of some very dedicated people involved. To those people, I will find you and I will thank you.

In true Paracon Australia style the magazine we've put together here is no different. What started as a spark of inspiration quickly turned into a mad dash to meet deadlines and put something that expresses all the ideals I have for the conference. One name I will call out is that of my wonder women graphic designer Nicola McIntosh who held my hand through this dizzy vision and turned a very loose idea into the magazine you are holding right now.

The magazine was put together the same way I approach and produce the conference (and even Ghosts of Oz podcast). I want it to be a thought provoking yet enjoyable experience. GOO, Paracon Australia and now this magazine is an exchange of ideas that really isn't after definitive answers but instead adopts the "strive for better questions" philosophy and hope it will generate further discussion and exploration.

Thank you to all the contributors who researched, interviewed, wrote and submitted work to this project. This is the part where I call out some highlights but in all honesty I encourage you the reader, the explorer, to approach it all and see where this adventure takes you.

Jump

Alex Cayas

Paracon Team

Alex Cayas : **EDITOR**
Alioth Poon, Peet Banks : **PRODUCTION TEAM**
Nicola McIntosh, Alex Cayas
Anne Rzechowicz, Mark Wallbank : **CONTRIBUTORS**
Scott Podmore, Josh Langley, Peet Banks, Rob Morphy,
Kerrie Wearing, Solreta Antaria, Jacqueline Anderton,
Beth Luscombe, Dan McMath, Amanda Moloney
Nicola McIntosh : **GRAPHIC DESIGNER**
inSpirit Publishing : **PRINTING**

Ben Hanson

Robert Murch

Peet Banks

CONTENTS

3 **OUIJA DOWN UNDER!** *The Good, The Bad and The Murch* By Anne Rzechowicz

5 **PROFILING BEN HANSEN** by Peet Banks

6 **PARANORMAL GIRL POWER** by Scott Podmore

10 **GETTING HAIRY WITH REX GILROY** by Mark Wallbank

12 **I HOPE I NEVER SEE BIGFOOT** by Rob Morphy

14 **AN OPEN LETTER TO ALL NON-BELIEVING SKEPTICS** by Kerrie Wearing

16 **PARACON 2014 YEARBOOK**

20 **COMMUNICATING BETWEEN WORLDS:** *Life as a Psychic Extraterrestrial Communicator* By Solreta Antaria

22 **ATTILA KALDY** *Validating the Paranormal* by Dan McMath

24 **FINDING THE SCIENTIFIC MEDIUM** by Jacqueline Anderton

26 **LOOKING UP FROM DOWN UNDER:** *The men behind "Australien Skies"* by Don Meers

28 **GHOST APPS AND WHY I HATE THEM** by Josh Langley

29 **PSYCHOLOGY** *Why is it not as popular with Paranormal Investigators* by Beth Luscombe

Cover image courtesy of The Carrington Hotel

Access Paranormal

Australia's chosen paranormal networking website

Paranormal Team Directories
Paranormal Event listings
Paranormal job opportunities
Recommended books
Equipment providers
Paranormal event co-ordination service
Monthly paranormal podcast

www.accessparanormal.com
www.facebook.com/accessparanormal
www.twitter.com/accesspara

OUIJA DOWN UNDER!
The Good, The Bad and The Murch

By Anne Rzechowicz (Eastern States Paranormal)

The year 2015 marks the 125th anniversary of the creation of the "Demon Portal to Hell"! Available in Barbie Pink Plastic or your traditional cardboard with Satanic symbols, at your local Walmart store! For us mere mortals, this is also known as the Ouija board. Whether you are a staunch believer of the evilness of the Ouija board or "it's a load of bollocks", it certainly stirs up passionate conversation and strong beliefs.

I had always been one of these people who was terrified of the Ouija board. Well, maybe not terrified, but I had a healthy respect for something I knew little about, except for the wild stories I had seen recounted in Hollywood movies. Part of me always thought "what if" it was a doorway, and I opened it, and I let something through that devoured my soul? How would I cram it back in its demonic box? Would I grow goat's hooves and horns? Would I lose my mind....any more than I already had? So many questions.

Last year I was lucky enough to attend Paracon Australia. I had gotten off a plane the day before from a five week paranormal road trip across America, and was determined to get to see the talk on Ouija Boards. I was compelled! So, suffering from a good dose of jetlag, I dragged myself off to Maitland Gaol and prepared for my eyes to be opened with actual knowledge and facts about the Ouija board. Robert Murch (the expert!) did not disappoint. He presented a fascinating history of Ouija: family feuds, Hollywood hype, town hysteria and religious fervour abounded!

So, what inspired Murch to start his obsession with Ouija boards? His Grandma of course! They used to love watching the old scary movies together and after watching Witchboard in 1986, his curiosity was piqued. Today Murch has over 500 boards of various shapes, sizes and nationalities. He is considered to be the expert in all things Ouija, and has been a consultant on several movies including What Lies Beneath, Sugar and Spice, Drive Thru and Winning Moves. Murch has also appeared and consulted for some of our favourite (or not so favourite in some people's minds) paranormal TV shows such as Paranormal State and most recently Ghost Adventures, where he talks about the dreaded Zozo!

Not only did Murch collect the boards, he also dug through the family history surrounding the creation of Ouija. It was enveloped in intrigue from its inception in the late 1890's. A family rift between brothers William and Issac Fuld ensued over the board, which lasted a century - and that is another whole story in itself (www.williamfuld.com). Murch brought the families back together again in 1997, a hundred years later, and the age old rift was healed.

The Ouija board has been blamed for many indiscretions during its time. The following story is an absolute cracker!

"The sleepy town of El Cerrito, California made the national news on March 7, 1920 with the headlines, WHOLE TOWN 'OUIJA MAD'. Horrified police arrested seven people 'driven insane' after using a Ouija board. One girl, only fifteen and found naked explained it was because she could 'communicate better with the spirits.' In the following days, the madness spread to others in the town including one police officer who ripped off his clothes and ran hysterically into a local bank. Officials quickly held a town hall meeting and decided to bring in mental health professionals to examine the entire population of 1200. To prevent any future outbreak of 'ouijamania,' they made the rational decision to ban Ouija boards from the city limits."

Darrin Langbien Photography ©

[source: http://www.museumoftalkingboards.com]

I remember a recent story in the news, claiming a teenage girl was "possessed" by a spirit from the Ouija board. There were controversial headlines around the world and people up in arms at the evilness of the board. After a little more digging, it turned out the girl had actually ingested some sort of substance that was meant to induce hallucinations. So, my question, was it the spirit through the Ouija board or the drug coursing through her veins that caused the "possession"? Was it an actual possession or simply hysteria on behalf of the people involved?

Personally, I think there is a lot of misunderstanding regarding the Ouija board. How easy is it to do something you shouldn't and claim "the ouija board made me do it!"?

Now, I'm not claiming carte blanche on the board, but I do suggest getting all the facts before loudly declaring DEMON!

Since attending Murch's Ouija talk, I have started collecting Ouija boards myself. My favourite is one from the early 1900's with its original wooden planchette. I have used it a couple of times and, I am relieved to say, so far I have not sprouted horns and hooves.

Personally, I believe Ouija boards are a legitimate tool for spirit communication. As with all otherworldly communication, you should handle it with a certain amount of respect. Sit with someone who is experienced, learn the rules and etiquette and have a good healthy dose of common sense! To me, it's a bit like handling a gun. What are your intentions? Do you plan to use it for mischief or dark deeds? Remember, like attracts like, so don't give it to someone who is drunk, on drugs or hysterical - you are only asking for trouble.

Australian
Paranormal & Alternative
Media

product promos
workshops
self promos for spiritual practitioners

Events Groups

Businesses

MOONLARK

Profiling BEN HANSEN

By Peet Banks

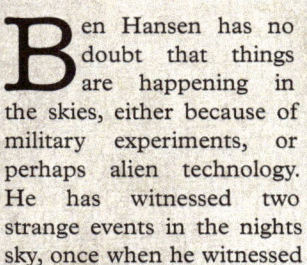
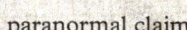

Ben Hansen has no doubt that things are happening in the skies, either because of military experiments, or perhaps alien technology. He has witnessed two strange events in the nights sky, once when he witnessed an object the size of a satellite travelling in a straight line over the Caribbean before making 'S' shapes, and another time in Utah when he saw an object moving in one direction before disappearing, and reappearing in another direction, and then taking off at 14 miles (17km) in only 4 seconds.

It was his fascination of the paranormal world, which stemmed from his love of the movie E.T. as a child that encouraged him to create SyFy's Fact or Faked: The Paranormal Files. Ben had been investigating with a group of friends when he heard that a production company was looking to create a paranormal show. They brainstormed, discussing the shows that were currently on TV and what elements they felt were lacking from those shows. From there the show was born. The premise of Fact or Faked is that Ben Hansen and his team set out to prove if an unsolved mystery has any basis in reality or not. Topics covered include the Sasquatch, the lunar landing, spectral visits and many alien/UFO visitation claims.

Outside of the paranormal, Ben built a career working with several investigative agencies, including as a Special Agent with the FBI, a position he held for six years, investigating child sex crimes and severe physical abuse on the Utah County Sex Crimes Task Force. He is passionate about serving the public and putting criminals behind bars, a commitment which no doubt originates from his upbringing.

Growing up in Utah, the second oldest of six kids, Ben's parents supported and encouraged him to pursue anything he wanted to do – from athletics training to piano and trumpet lessons. Ben had a diverse range of interests and an obsession to try new things, including becoming a licensed pilot, a licensed falconer, a certified hang glider and SCUBA diver, a search and rescue dog handler and an amateur radio operator – to name a few.

Ben believes that his training as a Special Agent has assisted him with his paranormal research, in that he has developed a methodical approach, much more so than most people. When undergoing an investigation, Ben writes reports and logs evidence, just as he would have as an agent, thereby enabling future investigators to view his reports and evidence to see if a particular phenomena may have happened previously, or perhaps have been debunked in the past.

After years of investigative work, Ben believes his skeptical side has been developed, in that he definitely needs to research a case completely before he will make a determination of a possible paranormal claim.

2015 marks Ben's second year as being a guest speaker at Paracon Australia. This visit will see him touring the country to investigate some of Australia's most haunted locations and going on a Yowie hunt, as well as conducting workshops and determining reliable UFO reports.

Paranormal GIRL POWER

By SCOTT PODMORE

We all know that men are from Mars and women are from Venus, and only the universe knows the truth behind why female-run paranormal tourism businesses are thriving in Australia. Watch any related TV program or tune into a radio show, and it's obvious the female energy plays an integral part.

As a small boy, my mother always told me to "have a girl's look" every time I struggled to locate something in my room. These days my wife tells me to have a girl's look. So, too, does my office manager, a woman of 60 who possesses impeccable attention to detail.

And it's that attention to detail that is just one of many reasons why women can be great business operators, especially when it comes to this type of work. A female business head and perspective creates that secret recipe in a paranormal tourism operation … a woman's intuition.

"Woman certainly bring a different viewpoint to the field," says Renata Daniel of Newcastle Heritage and Ghost Tours.

"Women are often more sympathetic and empathic and can have more 'feeling' experiences whereas often men are very black and white and don't muck about with how they describe what they encounter.

"I actually love listening to men describe their experiences," she continues. "Usually they are not embellished, they're just straight forward facts. Ladies love to add to the story, not because they want to make more out of it but just because that's the way we think."

Peet Banks, of APPI Ghost Hunts & Tours in Sydney, is on the same page.

"Without typecasting, and from my experience only, I believe women have better organisational and long-term planning skills," she says. "Obviously this isn't always the case, but in many instances men want to go and get their hands dirty and get the work done, without really caring how the event may have come to be. Whereas women actually organise it and make it happen."

So, when it comes to ghost tours and paranormal events throughout Australia, who you gonna call? Stick with these four women, who between them are experienced in paranormal workshops, theme nights, media work, ghost and history tours and more.

After all, when it comes to discovering ghosts and anything otherworldly, you can rest assured they'll be having a girl's look.

Beth LUSCUMBE
ACCESS PARANORMAL
www.accessparanormal.com

WHY THIS?

Believe it or not, it was the lack of events and information I couldn't find when I moved back to Australia from living in the United Kingdom. I had always had an interest in the paranormal but when I moved to the UK, I discovered that there were events, workshops and investigations that you could attend which were being run by other paranormal teams. They were interactive and educational which was due to paranormal shows becoming popular around that time (yes, I was one of those avid Most Haunted fans).

But after moving back to Australia I was enormously disappointed that there was hardly anywhere you could learn or experience what it was like to investigate the paranormal.

Luckily I was able to join a paranormal team for a year and a half and in that time I also launched Access Paranormal, which is aimed at paranormal investigators in Australia. It was initially a place where people could find information about events around the country but it has soon since turned into a focal point for the paranormal field with paranormal team directories to paranormal job opportunities.

WHAT SETS YOUR BUSINESS APART?

Access Paranormal is different for many reasons. It's information for the Australian Paranormal Investigator and although there are many great websites out there for investigators around the world, there isn't anything just for the Australian paranormal field.

Access Paranormal is also run by a person who is an investigator within the field who also has training and assessment qualifications. Knowing your market, what it deserves and what you can provide is the key.

BUCKET LIST PARANORMAL SPOOKY LOCATION IF YOU COULD?

Waverly Hills Sanatorium in Kentucky, USA. It's so iconic and one I would love to explore.

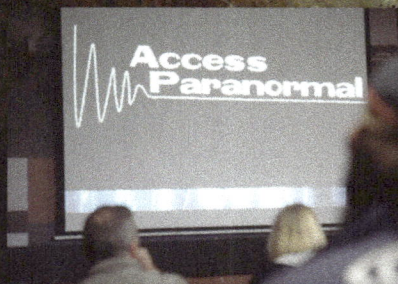

Renata DANIEL
NEWCASTLE HERITAGE & GHOST TOURS
www.newcastleghosttours.com.au

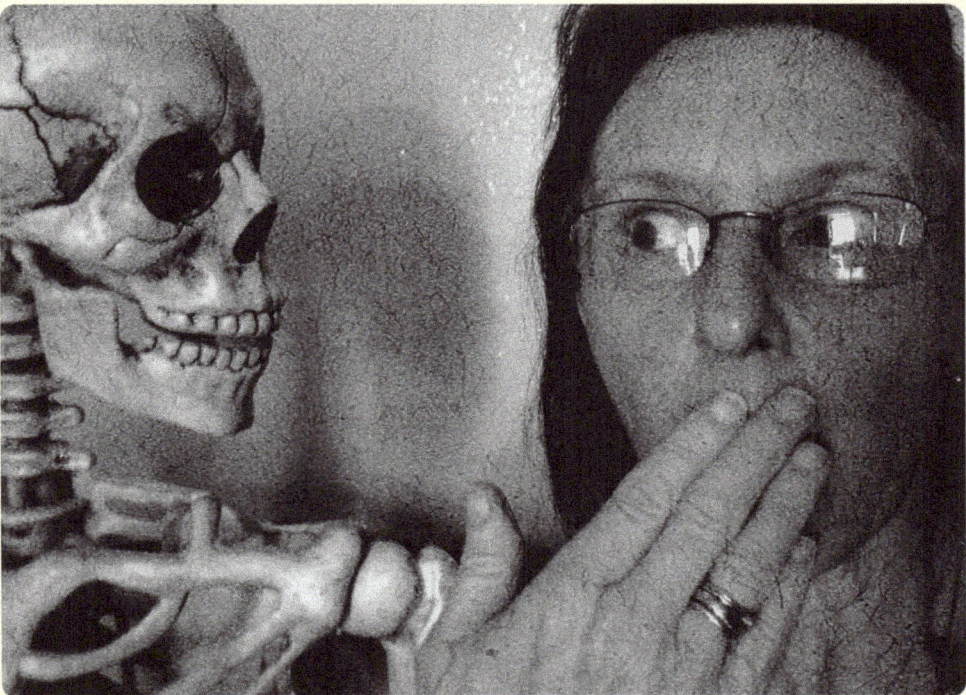

WHY THIS?

I've been drawn to the paranormal for as long as I can remember. As so many others who have had childhood experiences, I too found myself suffering from nightmares/visitations that, as a toddler, frightened the life out of me. As I didn't know how to even explain these things it was a matter of my parents trying to settle a child who seemed to just have an unusually nervous disposition and nothing more.

But, the fascination with all things spooky followed me as I grew and even those first formative years filled with night terrors didn't seem to deter me. I was always labeled as 'different' but had many years of a normal life marrying and having two children.

As they got older I started to develop my own psychic abilities by learning tarot and study started in earnest. At 56 I am probably one of the older breed of ghost hunters in Australia doing their thing right now. With so many younger people now in the mix I am possibly considered rather old school in many of my views and methods but my passion for research and investigating has not waned in all the years that I have been exploring the paranormal. In fact, it's stronger now than ever!

WHAT SETS YOUR BUSINESS APART?

I am based in Newcastle, NSW, the second-oldest settlement on the east coast of the Australian mainland. It was started as a convict settlement, a place that was seen as an open-air prison and repository of the worst of the worst offenders in the colony in Sydney. Our history dates back to 1804 and the first 20 years its all about the convicts and the military that ruled their lives.

The history of Newcastle is totally thrilling and amazing. When I first started to consider creating tours and creating a business, I did a lot of research and spent many hours walking the streets finding myself being followed by a few of the ghosts that I now talk about. As the tours started and the years have passed I have a great collection of stories shared by those who call me, email me or come on tour and tell me about their own personal encounters with our local ghosts.

Our tours are a mixture of history and storytelling and take people to the sites and spots where the ghosts of Newcastle lived, worked and died.

We also try to provide an atmosphere of learning rather than just plain entertainment during our tours trying to explain to people that investigations and paranormal experiences don't always look like what they see in the movies and that demons do not hang in every dark corner ready to pounce.

BUCKET LIST PARANORMAL, SPOOKY LOCATION IF YOU COULD?

I have always wanted to travel to England and Scotland to experience some of the old sites there and am happy and excited to say that I will be doing just that very soon. I will try to fit in as many old and historic sites as humanly possible. I will be sharing this on my blog and also on my Newcastle Ghost Tours Facebook page.

PEET BANKS
APPI GHOST HUNTS & TOURS
www.appighosthunts.com

WHY THIS?

I came into the paranormal field as an absolute believer. My grandmother had passed away a year or so beforehand and I was grieving. I attended a few tours, met a few people and did my research. Eventually my friend Nic Hume and I decided to form our own team, and APPI – Australian Paranormal Phenomenon Investigators – was born.

I have learned so much since then and I cringe when I look back at myself during that period of time, but at the same time I understand that everyone has to begin somewhere, and I have definitely learned from my experiences. Nic and I now run successful paranormal-themed nights at venues across NSW.

WHAT SETS YOUR BUSINESS APART?

We like to stretch our legs and venture into more than just ghost tours and paranormal investigations, so we have started to make our events 'theme nights'. We hold 'fear challenges' and unusual experiments – such as paranormal themed scavenger hunts and urban legend debunking. Although I would not consider myself a spiritual person, we also incorporate a spiritual aspect to our events, as we know there's a market for it.

We are also the organisers of the Australian Paranormal and Spiritual Expo, which is on to its third year. This event just keeps growing and growing and we look forward to bringing it to the public for many years to come.

BUCKET LIST PARANORMAL, SPOOKY LOCATION IF YOU COULD?

I am a lover of history and a lover of the ancient world. There are so many places I would love to visit. The Pyramids, the Great Sphinx, the Ajanta Caves in India, the 800-year-old cliff dwellings in Colorado, the Vatican Vaults – who knows what treasures you would find inside those vaults. I've always believed that if past lives exist, it's possible that we once lived in those places that we have the most interest in.

ALISON OBORN
ADELAIDE HAUNTED HORIZONS
www.adelaidehauntedhorizons.com.au

WHY THIS?

It started with my being born into a haunted house in England. My earliest childhood memory is of the sound of laboured/raspy breathing in the bedroom with me when nobody was there. My second, my brother's clockwork toys starting up around me when I sneaked into his bedroom to play with them (he always had the fun toys). The house terrified me, but it was like a moth to a flame and I found myself drawn to the subject all my life. It wasn't until I came to Australia in 1989 that I took up seriously investigating. I wanted answers but not at the expense of lying to myself that it was all paranormal. I was quite happy to find a natural explanation.

Not being satisfied with the way it was being done in other teams we were in at the time, a couple of us realised that the only way we could do it the way we wanted it done, was to set up our own team. So in 2002 Paranormal Field Investigators was born. We were lucky to be allowed into the Old Adelaide Gaol on the same year to investigate. We intended to do only three months and then move on, but it ended up a 10-year investigation, all of which was written up in my book Ghosts of the Past.

About the same time we helped develop the Gaol ghost tours and started guiding. Being able to share my passion for history and for the paranormal with others blossomed over the years and led eventually to setting up my own tourism business, Adelaide's Haunted Horizons. I was surprised how well it was embraced by both the public and the tourism industry, culminating in receiving a bronze and silver medal in the State Tourism Awards. I have plenty to thank our original ghost 'Mr Miller' for, especially for having set me on my path.

WHAT SETS YOUR BUSINESS APART?

A few things. Firstly, it's the staff ... the beating heart of Haunted Horizons - it is difficult to describe in words, but our relationship and how we obviously enjoy working with each other does rub off on the tours. We choose people who have a sense of fun and although they take the work seriously, not so much themselves.

Secondly, we understand that you don't have to have something happen to be able to enjoy a ghost tour. Some other tours feel the need to put things on and embellish, because they have a misconception that the guests won't enjoy or come back if they don't. We have proven this simply isn't true. If you don't insult the intelligence of the guests, and keep it honest, it is much more appreciated. "Keeping it real" is our motto.

Thirdly, without a doubt, we have worked hard in gaining the trust and respect of some of the top venue owners in South Australia. We now operate in some of the most haunted locations in Adelaide including the National Railway Museum, Adelaide Arcade, Ayers House and our most notorious venue, Old Tailem Town Pioneer Village. We have another to bring back to the stable ... so stay tuned.

BUCKET LIST PARANORMAL, SPOOKY LOCATION IF YOU COULD?

Definitely Waverley Hills Sanatorium in Louisville, Kentucky.

Getting Hairy

with REX GILROY

N.Z Paranormalist, Mark Wallbank chats to the Grandfather of Yowie research in Australia

Rex Gilroy, Director of the Australian Yowie Research Centre, Katoomba, NSW studying the Wadbilliga Dryopithecine fossil footprint. It is yet one more piece of evidence of an Australian primate presence in Pleistocene times and earlier. Photo copyright © Rex Gilroy 2013.

I first heard about Rex Gilroy as a child. Perhaps about 1980, or thereabouts. I was a budding young cryptozoologist / paranormal researcher that would spend my time reading up every book or article I could find on the subjects. I also collected newspaper clippings. In my collection I have clippings that mention Rex Gilroy. His explorations around Australia, and more importantly to me, his trips to New Zealand in search of lake monsters, the elusive hairy Moehau and following up on sightings of a group of moa reported to be living in New Zealand's densest forest ranges. To me, he was a real life Indiana Jones. I wanted to be like him. I made it a goal to meet this guy one day. Meet, talk and, if the planets were in alignment, explore with him.

Fast forward to Paracon Australia 2014. I was asked to do a talk about NZ cryptids. I was excited, nervous and honoured. Then I read that Rex was on the bill. The goal I made as a child was actually going to happen!

….and here we are again; Paracon Australia 2015. Rex and myself are both on the bill. Rex has promised to take me out exploring afterwards, and I've been asked by the Director to do this magazine interview with him …..yep, life sure is good right now!

So Rex, tell us a bit about your childhood and life growing up. Can you remember the moment when the yowie spark ignited and your obsession started?

I grew up on a farm on the Georges River at Lansvale, outside Cabramatta [born Nov 8th 1943]. The area, 30 kilometres south-west of the Sydney CBD and now built on, was then an area of farms and bushland and it was in the bush that I became fascinated by insects and spiders by the age of seven. This led me to collect insects, then rocks, which I kept in shoe boxes. At primary school I read all the books I could find in the school library concerning insects and native animals. Going to Liverpool Boys High School in 1957, I continued my interests and by now had learnt how to collect, record and display insects and spiders. Meanwhile, whilst still very young, my dad used to tell me stories of his youth. Growing up in Scotland, the ruined castles, and 'Nessie'. By High School I had become interested in archaeology and mystery animals as a result! The school library contained old books on the Aboriginal myths and legends among which was one with tales about the Hairy man, or Yowie, to which I was immediately drawn.

In the past you've been labelled "eccentric", and some of your methodology and theories have been put to question by people with differing views. I for one love this quirk in people and consider myself a little eccentric in my own way too. But do you feel this label is justified, or is it just a matter of being misunderstood?

'Eccentric' I may be, yet if I were not, I would not have been able to accomplish all the great discoveries I have made in a lifetime's research. I have gathered the largest privately owned natural science collection in Australia, in the course of which I have made many important discoveries. Being an amateur, it is only natural that the conservative university-based scientific fraternity of 'desk-professors' criticise my 'methodology' and theories and my many jealous rivals frequently attempt to discredit me with many untrue statements and attacks which have become quite slanderous at times. The trouble with these people is that, unlike them, I steer clear of sensationalism - ie organising well-publicised media-backed 'Yowie hunts'.

Your theory on the yowie as being a direct relative of Homo Erectus; has this always been your conclusion, or has this changed through the years as evidence has been found?

As my book *The Yowie Mystery – Living Fossils from the Dreamtime* demonstrates, I have given scientific credibility to Australian relict hominin/Cryptozoological research. My jealous rivals have no credibility. So they attempt to have me pushed aside from the very research that I founded back in 1957. I have revealed the 'Fossil Foundations' of Australian relict hominology. By presenting a wide array of fossil remains I have shown that the Yowie is a composite creature of ancient Aboriginal traditions, consisting of four races – a giant-size and average modern human form of living Homo erectus as well as a pygmy race, ie the 'Little hairy people'. The Yowies, or 'Hairy People' were called such because

The Giant Australian Monitor Lizard, Megalania prisca Owen. Supposedly extinct at least several thousand years, modern-day sightings claims of this reptilian nightmare persist. Sketch copyright © Rex Gilroy 2006

A preserved specimen of a Tasmanian Tiger, or Thylacine on display in the Western Australian Museum, Perth. The Thylacine displayed here is exactly the same as one seen by Rex Gilroy outside Blackheath NSW, on the night of Tuesday 22nd February 1972. Photo taken by Rex Gilroy at the Western Australian Museum, Perth WA.

The "Australian Panther", this sketch by Rex Gilroy, based upon eyewitness descriptions shows the animal to possess dog-like head features. These marsupial carnivores are a probable relating species of the 'extinct' Marsupial Lion, Thylacoleo carnifex'.

The fossilised Tyrannosaurid footprint discovered by Rex Gilroy in Sydney's Kuringai National Park on Wednesday 5th May, 2010. When it was first discovered filled with leaf litter. Photo copyright © Rex Gilroy 2011

Rex Gilroy with casts of some of the many Yowie footprints from his collection, together with others from South-east Asia, China, Russia and North America. Photo copyright © Rex Gilroy 2013.

Rex Gilroy, Director of the Australian Yowie Research Centre, Katoomba, NSW studying the Wadbilliga Dryopithecine fossil footprint. It is yet one more piece of evidence of an Australian primate presence in Pleistocene times and earlier. Photo copyright © Rex Gilroy 2013.

of the marsupial hide garments they wore/wear. Being Homo erectus they also know the manufacture of fire, stone, bone and wooden implements. The fourth race is something else, a primitive ape-like form that lives on an herbivorous diet and is not a toolmaker or fire-maker. The physical features of this race I have compared with those of Australopithecines. I possess fossil skull-types from Australia to back up my claims. My rivals have not one piece of scientific evidence to back up their so-called 'research'. None of them have any grounding in primate/hominin anatomy or physiology. To be precise, they are on a dead-end trip to nowhere.

I've always loved your incredible energy and passion for this field and have to say you've been a huge inspiration to me, so it was a thrill to finally get to meet and spend time with you after years of following your extensive research work. I've always appreciated your honesty, in stating that your theories on cryptids are just that, theories. Letting the reader come to their own conclusions without forcing unverified facts at them to blindly believe. So many researchers out there publish theories as absolute fact, which I think is wrong.

I am often ridiculed for my theories, but I go in search of evidence to support them. I have always kept an open mind on any phenomena and tell other people to do the same. I always say. *"This is my theory on [whatever subject], what do you think".*

Do you feel the Cryptozoological field is heading on the right track or could things be done better or differently to aid its progression?

In Australia relict hominology and Cryptozoology are unfortunately largely in the hands of the idiot fringe just described, but there are, apart from Heather and I, good people who think as we do, and want to get rid of the sensationalising, media-hunting element. We prefer to conduct our research in as scientific a manner as possible. Only this will ever win the approval, and at least open-minded respect of the university fraternity. No-one can say that I have not carried out my research and gathered evidence in a sensible scientific manner. This is why the Gilroys have so much evidence and our critics none.

You've been to New Zealand a few times in search of everything from the Moa, mysterious lake beasts and our own version of Bigfoot, the Moehau. What would you consider your best or favourite piece of cryptid evidence gathered from New Zealand?

At 71, I am still actively pursuing all these fields of research that I love. The word 'retire' is not part of my vocabulary. My favourite piece of cryptid evidence from New Zealand? The list is quite long. I have uncovered crude 'dawn tools' or eoliths of Homo erectus form North and South Island Pleistocene sites dating back 400,000 to 555,000 years BP [Before Present]. Footprint casts of the Moehau match Yowie examples. And both match fossil footprint impressions left by Homo erectus in Australia. Homo erectus, our immediate ancestor, walked into NZ from Australia over a former land-shelf that once joined Australia and New Guinea to New Zealand, itself part of the former Asia-Australia land-shelf which was covered by rising oceans 15,000 years ago, and of which only islands remain. I also possess three skull-types of pre-Polynesian origin dating back 500,000 years or more. Aside from hominin evidence, I possess a 2 million year old mineralised moa skull, and casts of Moa tracks. I treasure these relics for they were found by me in my favourite country beyond Australia.

Youve built up quite an impressive back catalog of written books on everything from UFOs, to Yowies to ancient civilisations. Any new publications on the horizon?

I'm planning books on our New Zealand searches. Meanwhile I have published quite a number of books so far, and recently completed my memoirs. Our next job is to put a book on the Hawkesbury River Monster on disc, get it to the printers and out on sale. I have three other books on the Yowie, a book on the Thylacine, the Moa, three UFO books among others to be put on disc and off to the printers in due course. I also have three books on the Uru Civilisation and another of mediaeval European exploration of the Australia-New Zealand-Pacific region to publish. And on it goes….

This year is proving to be a big one for discoveries. I have just uncovered fresh Yowie footprint evidence in the Kanangra wilderness and since January have uncovered pygmy fossil skulls dating back around 1 million years.

This man is a living legend. Passionate, unstoppable and perhaps a tad eccentric. But eccentric in that confusing, but incredibly intriguing and fascinating way. I'd love to spend time in this guy's head for a few hours. I'm sure it would be an incredible journey! I look forward to reading and hearing about further adventures with this seasoned and time tested yowie explorer, Rex Gilroy.

Rex at his former Tamworth NSW Natural Science Museum. Photo copyright © Rex Gilroy 2013.

BIGFOOT: GENTLE GIANT

AMERICANMONSTERS.COM — ROBMORPHY.COM

I hope I never see Bigfoot. Well, at least not face to gargantuan face. Maybe if I was riding in a dirigible or a helicopter or a fully functioning Sherman tank, but the last thing in the world I want to bump into while wandering around in a primordial, shadow shrouded forest nestled miles away from civilization -- armed with nothing more than a compass, a canteen and some bug-spray -- is a 7 to 9 foot tall, 600 lbs. feral primate… thanks, but no thanks.

I know this might sound strange coming from a guy who has dedicated the better part of his adult life to fulfilling his childhood ambition of globetrotting, talking to eyewitnesses, researching and illustrating some of the most bizarre cryptid reports to come down the proverbial pike. A big, bearded bastard who -- fourteen short years ago -- co-founded American Monsters over a lunch consisting of nothing but red meat and pitchers of Belgian beer… it is, however, the simple truth.

Now don't get me wrong. I'm not harboring some highfalutin ideas about how precious universal mysteries are to the psychological and sociological framework in which we all co-exist; even if I do happen to agree with that assertion. Nor would I be so bold as to suggest that there are (or are not) supernatural elements about tales of hairy wild-men -- which have emerged from nearly every corner of the globe from Australia to Siberia -- that smack of some universal truth about evolution and the human condition.

No, for me it's something much simpler than that… the idea of crashing into a colossal ape-like monstrosity scares the living hell out of me, and for good reason. These huge creatures are wild animals. Wild animals are always dangerous; especially when their young ones are around… or when you intrude on their territory… or when they are hungry. Especially when they are hungry.

For the better part of five decades now, many -- if not most -- Americans' have harbored a kind of shared Harry and the Hendersons delusion regarding Bigfoot. They perceive this massive, bipedal beast to be little more than a reclusive gentle giant; a kind of colossal teddy bear that dwells in the nebulous void between a spine-chilling campfire story and the biological world. I consider this collective misconception regarding the gentle forest giant to not only be fundamentally erroneous, but downright dangerous.

For the sake of argument let's suppose for a moment that Bigfoot is a real animal, which is an easy assumption to make considering the scads of photographic, video, DNA and print cast evidence that has been collected over the decades. Granting that these creatures exist, one must also assume that they are both strong and swift enough to capture their prey, yet cunning and elusive enough to evade even the most skilled and well armed trackers and hunters. Furthermore, there is every reason to assume that Sasquatch and its ilk are omnivorous. More than a few observers testified to seeing these ominous ape-men killing and eating deer, dogs, rodents and sometimes -- grisly as it may be -- even humans!

As if that weren't unsettling enough, there are multiple accounts of these critters scaring off ordinarily fearless apex predators like the Alaskan grizzly bear. Bearing this in mind, one is compelled to consider just how wise it would be to stumble into a region where even gigantic grizzlies and hyper-carnivorous wild felids fear to tread.

One need only glance at the published accounts of encounters with Sasquatch to find story after story of rocks being thrown at unwary travelers, or cabins ransacked by huge, two-legged scavengers, or monstrous hands reaching through the windows of rural homes, or pets found mutilated in the yard next to oversized humanoid footprints, or hikers who claim to have been pursued -- or in some cases even kidnapped -- by mammoth wild men who reeked of sulphur and rotten flesh.

In chapter 12 of his book Bigfoot! The True Story of Apes in America, noted author and cryptozoologist, Loren Coleman, chronicles the oft ignored side of primatology's most elusive quarry -- the slaughtering Sasquatch. The author states:

"Stories of violent Bigfoot do exist. Giant cannibals in the bush eating woman are part of ancient Indian lore… there are also reports of Bigfoot… killing dogs. These begin with the hairy giant 'Wildman' of Gladwin County, Michigan, who killed a dog with one blow of its hand, in October 1891, to… the 1970s

OR APEX PREDATOR?

seen carrying the bloody carcass of a dog. There is also the Wisconsin encounter in 2000 of a similar beast carrying a dead and bloody animal.

"Famed Bigfoot researcher John Green also collected stories of Sasquatch killing dogs and he dug up no less than six accounts of human beings who were murdered by Bigfoot. One of these harrowing tales hailed from Alaska during the 1970s. His informant told Green of a hairy, man-like beast that had attacked men who made their homes on boats anchored in the Yukon River. The account recorded that the boatmen's dogs managed to drive off the shaggy giant, but the injuries sustained by the men were more than they could bear, and they all died soon after.

Another disturbing account was published in the October 31, 1970, edition of the Bigfoot Bulletin by George Haas. Reprinted in that issue was a letter from an army trainee named Nick E.

Campbell, who was stationed at Fort Ord, California. He claimed that two Texas National Guard privates -- one of whom was a minister named Royal Jacobs -- told him that in 1965, a "giant hairy creature" had allegedly killed some people near Jefferson, Texas. The Reverend told Haas that he was a member of the posse that tracked the beast and that he had bore witness to the ravaged corpse of one of the creature's victims.

There is also the famous story recounted by President Theodore Roosevelt in his book The Wilderness Hunter, which was published in 1890, wherein two trappers had a ghastly encounter with a huge hairy creature in the Bitterroot Mountains. While one of the men checked the traps the other stayed behind to pack. When the first man returned, he discovered his partner's corpse. His neck was broken and four puncture wounds (probably teeth) had collapsed his throat. Needless to say the trapper wasted no time in exiting the area.

More violent antics occurred on August 13, 1965, when an enormous bushy beast attacked 17 year-old Christina Van Acker and her mother, Ruth Owens, in Monroe County, Michigan. Van Acker was driving her mother home when she felt a jolt. She hit the brakes and was immediately grabbed by "a huge hairy hand," which was connected to a growling, smelly, humanoid, who proceeded to slam Van Acker's head against the inside of the car door. Owens ran for help. It's a miracle that she ever saw her daughter alive again.

On July 16, 1924, The Oregonian published a story about group of miners who claimed they shot and killed an "ape man." During what must have seemed like an endless night, the miners were besieged in their cabin by enraged, rock throwing man-beasts that did their level best to break down the windows and doors. The men remained up throughout the night blasting holes in the cabin's walls in an effort to kill their simian assailants. The site of this incident was known as "Ape Canyon" from thereafter.

Another story seems to prove that these creatures are not just aggressive toward humans, but toward each other. The frankly disconcerting account comes form George Brusseau who wrote about a terrifying experience that this grandfather Elliott had while hunting with friends in 1944, in Okanogan County, Washington. Excerpted from his letter: "Grandfather Elliott was... hunting with some old buddies... when they happened on a terrible ruckus. They saw two big hairy males, each with their hands clasped together in club fashion, using them as weapons on one another; swinging their arms and clasped hands with full force knocking the other down until both were on the ground trying to get to their feet... The object of the disagreement appeared to be a dead deer. At one point the bigger Sasquatch... picked it up and swung the dead deer full force into the side of the face of the other hairy one... felling him to the ground."

Just to make sure we all full understand this astonishing situation; according to eyewitness testimony, one Bigfoot thrashed another Bigfoot utilizing a dead deer as a bludgeon. That ranks as one of the most awesome, terrifying and ostensibly true things I've ever read. Despite the disquieting undertones of their relationships with each other and the human race -- I will tactfully ignore accounts of Bigfoot having been caught mid-coitus with a presumably reluctant bovine -- it seems as if Sasquatch has got a crack public relations team.

Creatures that should inspire fascination in academic circles and awe and fear in the rest of humanity have become pop culture icons that have taken over the airwaves hawking everything from beef jerky to crackers and making regular appearances on reality TV shows too numerous to count. Midway through the second decade of the 21st Century, it appears as if this enigmatic entity has evolved from a incredible natural mystery to North America's unofficial furry mascot... and its popularity is growing exponentially.

Each year there are hundreds of Bigfoot reports from across the globe and probably twice as many that go unreported by those who fear being stigmatized as a fringe lunatic. But in the end, it's not the hearsay or the headlines that sends chills up my spine -- it's the stories that never get told... the stories that very likely die with their victims.

It's the backpackers who never come out of the forest or the hiker that official's claim must have "slipped" and fallen down a ravine, whereupon scavengers set in on the body. Events that get treated as unfortunate accidents or human error, when they could have just as easily been perpetrated by a pissed off, territorial alpha predator who gets off on turning human remains into Bigfoot chow... Of course, I might be wrong. Maybe Bigfoot likes to frolic through pastoral glade and nurse injured chipmunks back to life. I just don't know... and, with all sincerity, I hope I never get the chance to find out.

Rob Morphy artist/journalist/filmmaker/ designer/crypto chronicler/pod host and co- founder of .www.americanmonsters.com and

An Open Letter to all Non-Believing Skeptics

KERRIE WEARING is a Soul Coach, Medium and author of A New Kind of Normal: Unlock the Medium Within. She is Managing Editor of inSpirit Magazine, Director of inSpirit Publishing and currently working on her new book **Wisdom for the Soul.**

It is with heartfelt gratitude that I thank you for being you and not believing in Mediumship and what it is I do.

You see, because you exist I strive to be the best Medium I can be. I strive for more accuracy, more detail and I strive to deliver my messages from the Spirit world with statements, not questions. I also strive to keep my awareness of the non-believing public high at all times, for my fervent wish is that one day Mediumship will be accepted for what it is.

Right now at this point in time your view of Mediumship on the world stage is influenced by a select few and namely Mr John Edward. Your view is that John and many more like him are using cold reading techniques, not Mediumship.

John has proven himself time and time again and you only need to read the book, The Afterlife experiments, a concise scientific experiment on Mediumship conducted by the University of Arizona, to see this. This is one of the many experiments carried out around the world on Mediumship, yet it seems this fails to impact your thinking.

I do personally understand how you see a lot of Mediumship as cold reading. Many, many mediums with all levels of ability, some you'll even know, develop a habit of delivering their Mediumship with leading questions. For example: "Who is Fred?" or

Medium: "What does a blue car mean to you?"

Recipient: "Oh I just bought a new one"

Medium: "Oh great, cos Fred was just telling me that"

To me, it's not cold reading, it's just lazy and a Medium who actually has a weak link to Spirit. They got the Fred and saw a blue car, but that's it! They can't tell you any more about Fred, such as is he alive, dead, and is it the Spirit's name or the name of someone in the living the Spirit communicator wants to acknowledge. Nor can they tell you, what the Spirit communicator wants to say about the blue car.

A good Medium with a well developed link can and will elaborate, even extending upon the information. This style of Mediumship does lack in a lot of ways, and is fine when one is developing Mediumship, yet because we have no set Mediumship standard or governing body, Mediums too easily accept their current level of ability and get comfortable with what they know and how they do it. Preferring to stay here and allow the ego to rule, instead of walking with Spirit and going through the personal and spiritual growth it takes to keep extending and growing our Mediumship, which can at times be confronting and painful.

This however, doesn't leave Mediumship in a good light when it comes to how the general public perceives Mediumship, so recently when Chrissie Swan said to me on twitter "My behind the scenes experiences have been abysmal 9 times out of ten. In my opinion the majority of psychics and mediums do not have a 'gift'. I believe people must be very cautious. From what I have seen." And "If you had seen what I have seen you would be dismayed." I believe her. Chrissie is a radio announcer and former host of the Australian TV program The Circle, which has seen many of the well known international mediums appear on her show, including James Van Praagh, John Edward and Lisa Williams. We do however, have different views as to why this happens. Chrissie sees Mediumship as fake, while I see inexperience and ego as a much bigger concern.

This then leads me to question, what can we as Mediums do about this? For Mediumship to even to begin to be accepted more widely, we need to firstly stop making it out to be something special. It's not a gift, it's a talent that we nurture and develop just like anything else you aspire to be good at. Personally, I was not born with any noticeable psychic ability. I didn't see dead people as a child or make psychic predictions, yet 18 years after discovering my spirituality and mediumship, I am proficient at what I do because of years of dedicated training, attention and just doing it.

Secondly, we need to go about setting some global quality standards and regulate the industry in some way. A change such as this, needs to come from within the industry and right now the industry is too fractured a community for many to work together in harmony for one common purpose. So, having tried more than once myself, I know it will take someone with a profile and reach like John's or Lisa Williams' to affect this kind of change.

We can also keep striving to improve our Mediumship abilities and the information we are able to receive, and this is where you come in. I ask you as a non-believing skeptic to let me know what it is you need from us Mediums to believe. I invite you to comment, offer your thoughts and opinions. All serious comments will be considered, so just humour me and for the sake of it, pretend for a moment Mediumship is real and take the chance to have a constructive say. In broadening our view with an open dialogue you could be helping to evolve Mediumship to new heights. Come on! I know that a lot of you skeptics are highly intelligent people so your genuine input is valued.

With love and gratitude,

Kerrie Wearing

"This is an edited version of the original. To view the full letter please visit: http://www.kerriewearing.com/an-open-letter-to-all-non-believing-sceptics/"

> For Mediumship to even to begin to be accepted more widely, we need to firstly stop making it out to be something special.

paracon 2014 YEARBOOK
AUSTRALIA

Paracon Australia 2014 debuted its new look and new direction at the iconic (and riddled with ghost stories) Maitland Gaol, on May 10th and 11th 2014.

Paranormal researchers, investigators and enthusiasts descended on Maitland Gaol from across Australia and internationally, with guests travelling from as far as New Zealand and Las Vegas USA.

Speakers from every arm of the paranormal informed and inspired guests over the two days with lectures, screenings and workshops on wide topics, with everything from Yowies, Time Travel, Global Crop Circle Phenomenon, the Interplay of Media and Technology on Belief and OUIJASTITIONS – Ouija through the Ages.

Once the dusk hit, the spooky fun continued with our After Dark Events! Soul Conversations with Kerrie Wearing, Ben Hansen Investigation at Maitland Gaol Hosted Access Paranormal, and what has become the infamous Ouija Board Experience with Robert Murch and Jeff Belanger, where Murch and Jeff hosted over 80 people in a Ouija session in B-Wing of the Gaol.

The night continued with the VIP Investigation at Maitland Gaol with Ben Hansen, Jeff Belanger and Robert Murch with guests also having the opportunity to investigate with the Bill Chappell-modified Kinect camera.

INTERNATIONAL SPEAKERS included Ben Hansen (USA) as mentioned. Added to the list were; Author Jeff Belanger (USA) and Ouija board historian Robert Murch (USA), Investigators Mark Wallbank and James Gilberd (NZ)

AUSTRALIAN SPEAKERS included Kerrie Wearing (Author and Medium), Katrina Cavanough (Author), Mariana Flynn (UFO Research (NSW) Incorporated President), Attila and Andrea Kaldy (Filmmakers), Damien Nott (UFO researcher), Rex Gilroy (Author), Megan Heazlewood (Crop Circle researcher), Paul Cropper (Author), Irish Drummer Kevin Kelly

Communicating Between

Life as a Psychic Extraterrestrial Communicator

Growing up seeing and sensing spirits was just part of my everyday life. It was something that I was terrified of, as no one around me was experiencing anything like it, so it was just passed off as an active imagination. It wasn't until age 15 that my parents took me to see a Kinesiologist to help me with dyslexia. Only then did they take a deeper look into what I was seeing. The Kinesiologist said I was highly clairvoyant, and that I would become more so as I grew older. He recommended a friend of his who was a psychic teacher to guide me and suggested my parents enrol me in classes. But to my disappointment this was not to be, my parents preferring I finish school first. With the support of the Kinesiologist I stared to work through the fear, which enabled me to become more in-tune and work with the energies on a deeper level.

As an ET contact experiencer myself, I have had more than my fair share of experiences. Up until my 20's I found it extremely hard to get to sleep at night before 1am or 2 am, and often found myself surrounded by different beings as I would try to go to sleep.

Now that I am older, the beings will still come and visit, and a lot of the time they will appear beside my bed. My partner Peter Maxwell Slattery has often heard me communicating to Extraterrestrials in a sleep-like state, sometimes in English and sometimes in Star language. The good thing about having a partner who is a fellow experiencer is that we will often confirm what the other is seeing, without being asked.

It was still much later that I realised some of these beings were not from here and were from off-world and outer planetary locations.

A lot of people think UFO's are just lights in the sky, but we as humanity need to look past the physical side of this. There are intelligences behind these crafts, they are not just nuts & bolts.

Working as an ET communicator/Psychic I sense and communicate with vast array of different beings existing on various vibrations and dimensions, most of them living in a more subtle body than our own.

The one thing those aligned with our highest

Worlds

By Solreta Antaria

good have in common, is that most of them are here to work with us, helping to fulfil our life purpose or mission. They are working with humanity to bring about an awakening, showing us that we all have individual talents that can help humanity as a whole. They want us to move forward, to connect as one, and to think about what we do. They want all of us to shift through this awakening with the greatest of ease. They are trying to help us shift, and the more we can learn about them, the more we can connect and speed things up.

One of the things I do as part of my work is a combination of an Aura drawing and a Psychic reading. This gives each client a picture of the beings or guides working with them. With the picture, I also bring through valuable information and messages of why the beings are here, and on how they are connected with you. Each session is individually tailored and a lot of my clients have received information on their star lineage, and been given information on individual ways to connect with the Extraterrestrial beings around them. I look into deeper explanations on what's happening to them, and much more.

As part of my role being an ET communicator I speak Star language, some also call it the language of light. Although I can speak man star languages, I speak mainly a Sirian dialect which is connected to the star system Sirius. When I speak the language, it's not understood as a word for word translation. It's more understood on a telepathic/empathic level and often people who hear the language receive a feeling or a downloading of images or sensations on many levels. Examples of the language can be seen on my Youtube channel.

One of my favourite things about working in this field is every day I learn something new.

There are always new beings and star systems to be explored.

Solreta has appeared on TV & radio, she is a public speaker, author & teacher. She also has her own Youtube channel: https://www.youtube.com/channel/UCpCX1QzHA73kjE207lvXfExw/videos
For more information please go to: www.solretapsychicreadings.com
Or follow on Facebook : Solreta Antaria
Solreta is also part of T.A.L.K group Australia
www.talkgroupaustralia.com

ATTILA KALDY:

When talking about the paranormal here in Oz, there is one name in particular that raises more than a few eyebrows, and whose reputation in the Australian paranormal scene proceeds him. That name is of course Attila Kaldy. A man many of his peers refer to as 'The Godfather' of the Australian paranormal community. Now, I know this conjures images of an imposing figure reclining in a high backed leather office chair with a cigar in one hand and a KII meter in the other, but the reference is more about respect. In a field which here in Australia is still developing and growing, Attila leads the way in experimentation and research. His passion for all things unknown is what drives him. And his drive started at a very young age.

"When I was a little kid, (living just east of Bathurst NSW) I used to go out walking with my parents in the evening just after sunset, and my father and I would watch the night sky looking at satellites. One night we actually saw a satellite which was cruising, then stop, and then it did a 90 degree turn and took off. My father and I just looked at each other and said '…well that's not a satellite!', this was something a little more unusual." This was at the age 7. Not long after, Attila was given his first book on UFO's. The rest as they say is history.

Attila's account of witnessing an unusual aerial display was his first introduction into the world of strange phenomena. When he moved into a house years later in Europe, which was built in the 1920's by a Jewish couple who ended up being taken to Auschwitz in the 1940's, he was witness to ghostly footsteps, seeing the apparition of a man, and participating in his first séance. "I was about 14 or 15 and my parents were at work. So I invited some of my friends over and we decided to do a séance in the lounge room. Now nothing really happened, but when we went to open the blind, the blind just dropped down all by itself, which scared the shit out of us! Now whether or not it (the blind) was just sitting loosely or whether it was prompted by something else is another story." And that is how Attila and his wife Andrea, who formed the investigative body Validate, approach paranormal investigations. Analytical and above all, logical, which in this field, is paramount.

Moving into the new millennia, Attila branched out into media production, and in 2012, co-created Moonlark Media with Andrea. The production company, which specialises in visual content such as documentary making, focuses mainly on the spiritual and paranormal. After all, this is Attila's passion. For the paranormal devotee and investigator alike, there are some great offerings from Moonlark Media. The fantastic Paranormal Investigators Series 'Phasmophobia'(fear of ghosts) , My Project UFO and most recently an hilarious and slightly warped look at paranormal investigating with bite sized episodes of The Spook Troopers. And that's just the beginning! Attila and the team are currently working on a myriad of projects. There's the current Paranormal Investigators series 'In Tenebris', a journey into the darker side of the paranormal. The return of Phas, with Phasmophobia Resurrection, which we are told is something different to its predecessor, and a brand new series titled PI Uncut. Now with so many mainstream television shows available to the fan of all things paranormal, what sets these programmes apart from other paranormal shows? As Attila himself sees it, "……Well, the paranormal is extremely broad. It's not just about chasing shadows in dark corridors and people freaking out. It's a little bit more than that. What really draws me with content creation is the people that are in it! I'm more focused in the human experience of why people do what they're doing. This is why they, the viewer, can relate to the content, because it's another human being, in a very left of field situation."

Production isn't slowing down any time soon for Attila and Moonlark Media? Cue the upcoming Desolate! "Essentially, what we are doing is that the 3 of us (Attila, his daughter and a good friend of his) are taking on the lifestyle of homeless people, and we're going to these abandoned places in Europe. Old mansions and castles and what not, and we are going to stay a day and an entire night in these buildings, some of which are 600-700 years old, and see if history comes alive, and what we can get out of it in the way of hauntings and the like….I'm interested in soaking it (the history) up and connecting with the culture too…." The locations the crew will be calling home for 24 hours at a time are situated in a country with a thick history and have never before been investigated. The image of the promotional poster for Desolate, along with the premise of the production, already has a lot of us in the paranormal community salivating. We love this stuff!!!

It seems that the work Attila does with Moonlark Media is definitely a project of passion and it involves the whole Kaldy family! His wonderful wife Andrea (a paranormal medium…that's another article), his daughter Michelle and son Anikan, whom we know has a fascination with crypto-zoology…..and has a 5 kinds of awesome name! In the end, it's all about the journey. Attila Kaldy's path is one that every person who is someway involved or interested in the paranormal field, will benefit from. Attila, like anyone

Validating the Paranormal

else devoted to the paranormal realm, doesn't have ALL the answers, but he can sure make you think about the questions.

Make sure to come and listen to Attila at Paracon Australia 2015 presenting 'Back into The Woods. The Search for Australia's Bigfoot' and check out Moonlark Medias' productions on their youtube channels, and upcoming news on the Paranormal Investigators Series website.

Dan McMath is an co founder of Ghost Hunters Of the South coast & Terriortories (G.H.O.S.T.), the owner GHOST Paranormal Streetwear and recently joined the Ghosts of Oz podcast team as a co host and presenter.

Finding the Scientific

By Jacqueline Anderton

"... I try to remove all religious and spiritual components from mediumship and try to deal with mediumship as a function of a human being; whether it's a brain function, or a higher function."

In this age of Science where spirituality is seen as more of a health benefit than a mode of explaining reality, the Paranormal field has always seemed to exist in a theoretical 'no-man's land'. It seems to be located somewhere next to Kirlean Photography on the scale of scientific feasibility whilst caught in the reoccurring chorus of "I don't believe in ghosts, but…"

I do believe in the Paranormal, but I have noticed that science has – to all intents and purposes – become almost synonymous with truth; in that the scientific method mostly dictates what I eat, how often I eat it, how I sleep and what car I drive.

Even how I brush my teeth.

The definition of science itself is the intellectual and practical activity that encompasses the systematic study of the structure and the behaviour of the physical and natural world through observation and experimentation… So from this comes the question: why are we using it to explain the non-physical and supernatural world of the Paranormal?

Andrea Kaldy is a Paranormal Medium, a means of communication with the 'non-physical', the Paranormal, the supernatural. The things that we – as investigators – are attempting to track down in the darkness. She is a part of the investigative team 'Validate' and co-founder of 'Moonlark Media', an Australian film-production company dedicated to the production and release of Australian local Paranormal content.

She describes her Paranormal Mediumship as a tool like any other:

"I work with teams – I don't platform or do private readings – I work within their own framework whenever they want to research something or do their own experiments. I provide the mediumistic element if that is needed; [whether that is] correlations with equipment [or] personal experiences with the team."

"… I try to remove all religious and spiritual components from mediumship and try to deal with mediumship as a function of a human being; whether it's a brain function, or a higher function."

Even within the Paranormal field, the use of tools is a strange mix of the scientific and the psychic. It isn't all that rare to see a team with a 'Tech Manager' and a Medium; a representation of the scientific and the spiritual using the tools of their trade to investigate the unknown.

TV shows like the infamous (and slightly discredited) 'Most Haunted' and (not-so-discredited) 'Ghost Hunters' were the first to promote this blend of skeptic science and spirituality. This has since grown with the rising popularity of the Paranormal in media as the field seemed to embrace the scientific elements in investigating the supernatural.

Teams around the world have mostly started to mimic what has been popularised by American tv shows, with slight variations like the use of a mobile lab in Discovery's 'Ghost Lab' and minimalized crew in Travel Channel's 'Ghost Adventures'.

Bill Chappell is a not-quite-retired electronics engineer and inventor, who has produced some of the most unique and intriguing equipment used by Paranormal investigators around the world. His company Digital Dowsing is responsible for producing most of the equipment for the Travel Channel series "Ghost Adventures" since their inception in 2008.

"I would describe what I do as engineering; the creation of the devices [that I produce] are more a process of applying known processes to solve a problem."

"[I am] … Not really a spiritual person, I'm a skeptic in the Paranormal field. By that I mean I don't accept the standard principles applied by the community; I do not believe in ghost or spirits."

To the most devout t.v. ghost-hunter this would seem like blasphemy, but Bill has identified perhaps the greatest mistake that a lot of investigators in the field have made when investigating the Paranormal.

The standard principals applied by the community to the Paranormal have largely come from t.v. shows and media - one example being that ghosts are remnants of the deceased and that EVP's are 'voices from the beyond' - and may not necessarily be right.

"I've always been concerned with method rather than message," Bill says, "I don't just accept EVP as a disembodied spirit or a time slip or any of the popular theories out there. Til I understand the true origin the 'messages' are not meaningful to me."

"I don't call anything we get 'Evidence'. It's all interesting, but I don't see it as proof…

and I have always expressed that view."

The idea that a spirit or ghost is a remnant of the deceased gets its roots largely from the religious and spiritual belief that there is life after death. The assumption is that once we die, a small part of ourselves is separated from our bodies.

Andrea – in her work – acknowledges the risk with falling into the same popular Paranormal and religious assumptions when investigating the Paranormal.

"What if it's the blind leading the blind? If we're all going in the same direction how are we going to be coming up with new ideas if we're all following the same person, or school of thought?"

"Especially when we work in the Paranormal if we want to be taken seriously then – in my opinion – we have to remove all religious and spiritual elements… because they are very specific. They have their own framework and processes for [dealing with] the spiritual."

"You can have mediumistic or spiritual

Medium

experiences without any kind of religious or spiritual education or influence."

And so I return to my original question: how can we apply the scientific method to a field where the fundamental principals are unknown without falling into the trap of assumption, or relying too heavily on religious and spiritual frameworks?

The answer is… we don't know. The Paranormal field is still largely unknown, so we still have so much freedom when it comes to the way that we experiment and investigate. Why not take a little of everything? Build on others ideas - build on your own ideas - but don't be afraid to challenge them.

"Everybody has a reason for why they are saying what they are saying." Andrea says, "Everybody has a reason for why they believe what they believe. Whether they choose to disclose that reason or not, who am I to judge? To me the basis of the debate is mutual respect, not just towards each other as a person but towards each other's opinions."

Scientific and spiritual frameworks are just that; frameworks. They are ways to interpret Paranormal evidence – not necessarily ways to define the Paranormal.

"My personal goal is to solve 1% or maybe even .1% of the paranormal puzzle before I retire from the field." Bill says, "Proving even one small piece would ignite research and experimentation on a global scale."

"Someday, we may not have all the 'Science' needed to really understand all that goes on around us. There are many un-explained issues in physics such as a unified field theory, dark matter and many more. It will take time to reconcile the Mind, Physics and the Spiritual realm. I'm sure 100 years from now those 3 things will have much different meanings then they do now."

Bill Chappell

Looking up from

The men behind "Australien Skies"

By Amanda Moloney

For so long now Australia has had many reports of unidentified flying objects and strange lights. Many times the subject was kept quiet and not really played out in the media. However, the new documentary Australien Skies is a journey that the viewer gets to take part in. Renowned cinematographer and composer Don Meers follows Australian Ufologist Damien Nott around for 4 days to hopefully find answers to the phenomena he sees. Damien started to experience sightings when he was around 9 years old that led well into his adult life. He has been lucky enough to see unusual lights in the sky and craft like objects and currently has over 1800 photos and 200 videos showing lights, shapes and saucers.

Damien you say that you've been experiencing sightings since you were about 9 years old. What was it about these phenomena that drove you to 'research' as opposed to just "having" an experience?

DAMIEN: Originally it was my sighting at the age of 9 that made me interested in the phenomenon of UFOs, but what got me into researching were people's dismissive attitudes towards others who see UFOs. My mother had originally dismissed my own sighting as a plane so I actually wanted to show her that others around the world had seen the same things as me. At the time I did not understand why she did not believe me or dismissed my sighting, but then I found that it was an attitude that was entrenched in society in general.

Don what began your interest in the UFO side of the paranormal? Was it an actual event that happened or a gradual extension of other paranormal interests?

DON: I grew up in the Star Wars generation and loved all the Sci-fi and TV docos that were prevalent in that period. I'm fascinated by all the fringe genres Bigfoot, ghosts, UFOs and everything in between. But I am completely underwhelmed and exhausted by current paranormal reality television.

Where did the passion for creating documentaries come from? Have you always wanted to tell these types of stories?

DON: I started as a musician and the music that I liked to create was very visual/soundtrack orientated. Eventually the work I was doing in sound at the time started to stretch across to vision so it was all a very natural progression. As far as documentaries go, I love going on adventures and this style of film making, again, is very natural for me.

Why do you think that the upper end of Australia and outback areas seem to receive more UFO visitations than anywhere else?

DAMIEN: It does seem that certain remote areas seem to attract more UFO sightings than built up city areas. We do not know their motives and agendas so one can only apply human logic to attempt to answer this question. If we wanted to get away with doing something without being witnessed then we would do it in an environment without a built up population, so limiting the amount of people seeing what we do. Another thought on this is that they may be affected themselves by the negativity in built up areas like the city, so hence they prefer to keep to themselves as much as possible. People in larger populated areas such as cities tend to look straight ahead and not up in the sky. People tend to be busy with work and are stuck in shops or office buildings, going about their duties in a rushed typical city life kind of manner. Country people however tend to be more relaxed and even though there are less of them, they are people of the land and tend to be more observant of things around them. Another possibility could be that they are attracted to minerals such as quartz crystal which seem to run in large veins under a lot of country towns.

Do you think we are seeing an increase in UFO activity or is it simply a case of now we have the wide world of social media and everybody having a smart phone?

DAMIEN: There are more reports coming in now than ever from all around the world of UFO sightings. This may be due to the fact that social media has opened up a lot of people's minds to the possibility of visitation. Also the proliferation of mobile phone cameras

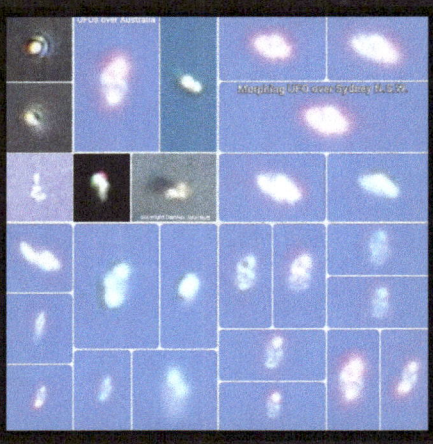

Down Under

enables people to photograph or film what they are witnessing. Speaking personally, there does seem to be a major increase in my own sightings so it does appear that something strange is going on in our skies.

DON: I'm not sure if we are having more sightings/experiences or if there are more outlets to relay ones experiences ie: social media etc. I think social media is playing a massive part in the data collection of the phenomenon nowadays.

During the course of working on your new documentary film Australien Skies what would be the most compelling piece of evidence you witnessed or heard about?

DON: Obviously we had a lot of footage from Damien which was fantastic but a real unexpected surprise for me came from another sky watcher we feature in the film by the name "Liam" Really close captures for long periods of time. It will make you rethink what is going on as it did me. Very, very weird! The thing that sets him apart from a lot of other watchers was that he really mastered his camera and utilised it to its full potential. Zooming right in on these objects and having stabilisation turned. It's going to blow a lot of people away as will Damien's footage.

What are you hoping to achieve with your documentary film Australien Skies?

DAMIEN: We are hoping to show that there is a phenomenon in our skies and that this phenomenon is interacting with people on this planet, people from all walks of life. We are not trying to show that they are little green men, but instead we are saying that we do not know what they are. The main objective is to open up people's minds to a greater reality that exists around us, one that has been denied and scoffed at for too long now.

DON: In general I'm hoping to push the boundaries in the genre. I am a part of a revolution of Australian paranormal film makers who want to be the very best in the world. We want to change everything. On a personal level I'm hoping to achieve personal satisfaction. I want to beat what came before. I want to get better at my craft and always jump up a level with each project. Each one of these films is practice for something bigger and better that I have my sights firmly set on.

Do you think that people are now more accepting that there is more out there than just us, for so long the paranormal industry, and particularly UFO research, has been ridiculed for the things it has believed in and studied?

DAMIEN: People are waking up now it seems to what is really happening above our heads and around us. There is a huge shift and change going on and the more people that witness the phenomenon, the more people will open their minds to a larger possibility that we are not alone out there. We are exiting the age of religion and entering the age of science, and even though the sceptics and scientists do not believe that alien life is visiting us, one day it will become common knowledge and our current paradigms will change. We as people are taught how to think and act from a young age through what we are taught in schools and society, when we break free of this programming and start to think outside the box for ourselves we will see that we do not know everything about the world and universe around us. We were once told and believed that we were at the centre of the universe and that the world was flat but we now know that these accepted beliefs in those times was flawed.

DON: I think people will believe what they need to believe. We have often attributed great mystical significance to things we don't fully understand but I think it really is going to be a waiting game as science starts to reveal new paradigms that challenge our old scientific, religious and social beliefs.

Ghost Apps and Why I Hate Them
by Josh Langley

Josh Langley is the Author of **Dying to Know: is there life after death.**
(Big Sky Publishing)
www.joshlangley.com.au

I'm a passionate afterlife explorer, but there's one thing about the investigation game I had been oblivious to, however I was soon about find out about it in near embarrassing fashion.

I'm talking about the Ghost App.

I had never heard of them, so wasn't looking out for anything dodgy when a friend sent me a private message on Facebook with an Instagram photo of her mum chatting to a friend at a picnic table. In very clear detail you can see the faint image of a young boy dressed in 1900's era clothing.

The background explanation was that the husband of the lady on the left had a new phone and was trying out the camera function and it just happened that the two ladies were talking about one of their dead brothers while he was doing it.

Yes, I thought it looked too real to be true, but I like to think the best of people and would wonder why anyone would want to prank me. Wisely I held back from posting the photo on the Dying to Know Facebook page until I could get it checked out. I should have known something was wrong when repeated requests to get the original photo from the husband were ignored.

So I ran it past a couple of mediums and they both said that they 'got something' from the image, and one even went as far to say the boy needed rescuing. Not wanting to get too carried away, I emailed Alex at Paracon for a level headed opinion and he alerted me to the Ghost app option, so I did a Google image search, and while I didn't find the exact little boy, I was shocked and disappointed that so many apps where out there, designed to trick and fool people, all under the banner of 'fun'. Now, I'm not a kill joy and wowser but it beats me how you can palm off such idiocy as fun?

I continued to scour the internet looking for my little ghost boy and still came up empty handed, until something truly bizarre happened. An old primary school friend, who I'd only seen once since school, messaged me on Facebook with "Hi Josh do u know the app called ghost in your photo." (sic)

I seriously thought she was referring to a photo I may have posted and she'd seen a ghost in it. I knew it couldn't have been the ghost boy one as I hadn't posted that, so I asked her to clarify what she meant and it then became clear to me she was referring to the app.

Back to Google, yet with a more targeted search and bang, there it was...the ghost boy sitting in among a collection of similar creepy images.

My long lost friend's seemingly random message lead me directly to the image, yet even more strangely, within an hour of receiving it, Alex had asked me to write a piece for the Paracon magazine and I knew instantly what I was going to write about, those bloody stupid apps!

It's already difficult enough to capture images of spirits, ghosts and energy forms and work out if it's not the end of some random cat's tail and then you add the a whole litany of ghost app photos on top of that, it just makes our job of finding the genuine thing even harder.

The general public becomes more sceptical and investigators then get fed up with people trying to 'show them up' with mindless tricks and idiocy. I know there's a long tradition of trying to scare the crap out of each other, that's why we subject ourselves to watching Paranormal Activity 8, but when as investigators we're trying to find evidence of life after death and show that there's a bigger reality out there, then it's a little disheartening to have the ghost apps getting in the way of real investigation.

While being a bit miffed about the whole thing, it only reinforces the main message I got while writing *Dying to Know: is there life after death* and which continues through the new book I'm writing. While we continue to look for physical evidence or evidence 'out there', we'll always be guessing, second guessing, making assumptions, drawing conclusions and being subjected to the idiocy of the human condition, but when we start searching on the inside for answers (personal experience, meditation, Lucid Dreams, OBE's etc) then a whole new world opens up, one that can't be downloaded from Apple for 99 cents.

Happy exploring!

Psychology

Why is it not as popular with Paranormal Investigators by Beth Luscombe

There are as many different ways to investigate the paranormal as there are many different areas of interest. The Paranormal isn't just the search to find possible evidence of the afterlife. There is also Cryptozology, Ufology, Survival Hypnosis (including NDE's), IR Theology, Demonology and the occult just to name a few.

But for argument sake, when investigating presumably haunted locations (or people) paranormal investigation teams generally tend to have members that specialise in either Technology/Equipment, Research/Historian or Medium/Psychic.

And one has to ask, do investigators these days explore psychology? Shouldn't we all be open to learning more of how our brains perceive information? How many teams have a person who specialises in this subject?

Dan McMath from Ghost Hunters of South Coast and Territories and team member of Ghosts of Oz Podcasts says: "Using basic psychology skills whilst on an investigation helps us separate what may be paranormal, and what we might think is paranormal. It's up to the investigator to question his own perceptions, as we all know, what we perceive to be real is open to interpretation".

Andrea Kaldy, Paranormal Medium and first half of Validate Paranormal and Moonlark Media explains "Psychology is often looked at as the poor cousin in science. Much like the paranormal. In that respect it's much closer to it than anything else. Paranormal events often have attributes that are specific to the observer and are unique to the experiencer, therefore puts it into a position where perception is the only, though scientifically unreliable, source of information."

So is that the reason why? It's hard if not impossible to measure a personal experience or personal interpretation of an event and therefore equipment and historical research is more reliable? Attila Kaldy who is the second half of Moonlark Media and Validate Paranormal explains it further "You know one thing many of us forget that any form of science literally discredits phenomenology and sees it as pseudo-science. Anything ambiguous in nature cannot be replicated or predicted even under controlled conditions. Science will never acknowledge anything that is considered ambiguous and immeasurable. Having said that, pursuing this field without having some knowledge of general science (psychology included) and wanting to make claim to a theory, in my opinion, is a death sentence".

Ok, so knowing some basic knowledge of psychology is important. But just because it's hard if not impossible to quantify or measure does that mean we push it aside?

I was fortunate to be able to attend the Australian Institute of Parapsychological Research's Annual Conference last year. There were a great selection of speakers presenting their theories and results of their experiments. But what surprised me the most was how many people showed up. It was packed and 90% of those who attended where not paranormal investigators nor a part of a team. Is it because the subject has the potential to be so intense? Would a Bachelor of Arts be needed just to comprehend the basics? Is the terminology alone just too confusing?

What if there was information available to help unscramble the complexity of this important area of information. Where would you go? Some experimental studies and research papers can be like eating a lemon – unpleasant. Luckily there are some institutions that do offer Parapsychology Courses that are easier to digest. Be wary though, make sure the institution has an accredited person who presides over assessing coursework. Research the qualifications of the person or people running these courses so you are fully aware of what you will be awarded after all your hard work.

If you are comfortable with essays then The Australian Institute of Parapsychological Research offer their online course "Certificate in Parapsychology" and "Certificate of Advanced Parapsychology" and are backed by some of the most well known Australian academics in the field (website link http://www.aiprinc.org/courses_online.asp).

But if you like something a little less "university" then Dr Ciaran O'Keefe offers his "Foundation of Parapsychology"(website link: http://theschoolofparapsychology.org/course.php).

The College of Management Science in the UK offer a Diploma in Parapsychology and this is backed by the Course Providers Association Accreditation [C.P.A.A.] (website link: http://www.unifaculty.com/html/paranormal_online_courses.html).

Knowing how that fantastic grey matter works is important for the field. Our brains are THE best paranormal tool that we've got so understanding how we perceive information, make decisions and decipher what we experience is an enormous advantage for all investigators.

Beth runs the successful website Access Paranormal. Having international paranormal investigation experience she has presented at Las Vegas Paracon, assisted Paracon Australia, consults on private cases, investigated locations interstate, co-hosted series In Tenebris (Latin for "into Darkness"), managed the Klinge Brothers Australian Tour and currently hosts successful podcast Access ParaCast.

WHITE Insurance Brokers
Proud GOLD Sponsor of Paracon Australia 2015

Paranormal & Supernatural Investigators Insurance

Tailored Insurance Scheme Specially For You

Activities automatically covered:

- Paranormal, Supernatural, Crypto-Zoology Investigations, Surveillance & Research
- Scientific Experiment, Assessment & Audit
- Audio, Electronic & Video Recording
- Data Collection & Transcription
- Medium, Psychic & Clairvoyant
- Secretarial, Administration & Office Support
- Training & Development
- Educational, Lectures & Seminars
- Workshops & Conventions
- Tours

Persons automatically covered:

Individuals, clubs, associations and businesses undertaking Paranormal & Supernatural activities and services with an annual turnover of up to $75,000.

$365
Per Annum*

Cover Limits:

$20,000,000
Public & Products Liability

$1,000,000
Errors & Omissions Liability

*Terms & Conditions Apply

For more information, please call **03 8790 5701** or visit our website:
www.whiteinsure.com.au/schemes-facilities/paranormal-supernatural-investigators-scheme

For all your Insurance needs

Accident & Illness	Construction	Hard to Place Risks	Management Liability	Products Liability
Business Insurance	Corporate Travel	Home & Contents	Marine Transit	Professional Indemnity
Business Interruption	Directors & Officers	Industrial Special Risks	Mobile Plant	Public Liability
Caravan & Trailer	Farm & Crop	IT Liability & Cyber	Pleasure Craft	Retail Insurance
Commercial Motor	General Property	Landlord & Strata	Private Motor	Workers Compensation

WHITE Insurance Brokers

16 Star Crescent, Hallam, VIC 3803 : T 03 8790 5701 : F 03 8790 5702
Email: info@whiteinsure.com.au : www.whiteinsure.com.au

White Group (VIC) Pty Ltd T/as White Insurance Brokers: ABN: 60 116 978 253 - AFSL & ACL No: 295436

www.ingramcontent.com/pod-product-compliance
Lightning Source LLC
Chambersburg PA
CBHW061539010526
44112CB00022B/2892